The Paranormal Chronicles presents

A most haunted house

By

G L Davies

The house first came to my attention a few years ago. I'd heard rumours of a prolific paranormal case that exhibited all aspects of a good haunting. It's always difficult when studying possible paranormal incidents to decipher fact from fiction and to explore the truth behind such talk. As always first dismiss rational explanations for the events. A birds nest in the attic and an over-active imagination can suddenly become a very real and frightening paranormal experience. Only when a thorough investigation has taken place, can an assessment be made. Often investigators in this field tend to be too open minded and fall foul of the power of suggestion and a desperation to prove that these things do exist. Whilst others are so sceptical that even if there were proof of a paranormal phenomenon they would simply dismiss the notion. It's all about balance and working through a series of processes. Eliminating the options until eventually you are left with (hopefully) either an explanation or, an event. Nine times out of ten it is something simple and mundane, but there are those rare cases when rational thought and science cannot explain what is happening.

One element of the story that did capture my imagination was, that the house and the people that lived there wanted to remain anonymous. Either this was nothing more than a spooky story with no substance, or something had been happening to the people and they wished it to remain private for fear of ridicule. In my experience, people don't wish for real incidents of paranormal phenomena to be made public. They have to live and deal with, what can be very confusing and frightening phenomena. People have approached me in the past claiming spectral, poltergeist or even alien activity. In reality, they craved attention and wanted to have the sense that something special was happening to them. Consciously or not, they were desperate for their existence to have more meaning and feel they had been chosen or selected by a higher unknown force.

A source gave me the general location of the property and to my surprise, I found it not to be some gothic or ancient looking building but a stereotypical street of terraced houses in Pembrokeshire in the centre of Haverfordwest. The area being mere minutes walk from local supermarkets, schools, shopping centre and amenities.

Haverfordwest serves as the market town for most of the county of Pembrokeshire, west Wales. It forms an important hub between other towns in Pembrokeshire such as Milford Haven, Pembroke Dock, Fishguard and St David's as a result of its position at the tidal limit of the western Cleddau River. The majority of the town, comprising the old parishes of St. Mary, St. Martin and St. Thomas, lies on the (west) bank of the river, whilst on the left bank are the suburbs of Prendergast and Cartlett. At this point, a pair of sandstone ridges extending east-west and separated by a deep, narrow valley, are cut through by the western Cleddau. This leaves two high spurs on the west side of the river. On the northern spur, the castle and its surrounding settlement form the core of St Martin's parish. On the southern spur, the High Street ascends steeply from the river, and forms the core of St Mary's parish. From the foot of each spur, ancient bridges cross the river to Prendergast: St Martin's Bridge ("the Old Bridge") and St Mary's Bridge ("the New Bridge", built in 1835). St Thomas's parish occupies the south side of the southern spur. From these core areas, the town has spread, mainly along the ridges. In addition to the four ancient parish churches, the remains of an Augustinian priory are visible at the southern edge of the town. Haverfordwest has a deep and rich history of folk lore and hauntings and even numerous UFO sightings during the

1970's that lead to the area becoming known as the Welsh triangle.

Some investigating led me to believe I had found the exact location of the house in which this haunting was said to have occurred. I was excited, but deeply anxious on how to approach the persons involved. I did not wish to seem overly presumptuous or assertive or to be viewed as obnoxious or to be deemed insensitive. I decided to simply write a letter, explain who I was and my background as an investigator. I explained that if they did have a possible haunting, I would very much like to investigate it. I assured them I would at all times respect their anonymity, and may perhaps be able to offer a solution or help them make sense of what was happening.

Two weeks went by and I had decided that perhaps, I had been misled or had mistaken the property for the one in the story. If that was the case, further research was needed to either confirm such a house did exist or to simply close the file as just an example of hearsay or urban myth. Then I received the email.

It was from a gentleman who had lived there at the alleged time of the incidents. He had been forwarded the letter and had mulled over the notion of an outsider wishing to scrutinise a very private matter and had needed to speak to the other people connected. He politely informed me that those involved, did not and would not speak to me and to never make any contact with the residents of the house or to mention his name. I replied, profusely apologising saying that my intent was of a scientific and investigative perspective rather than one of glorification or an attempt to exploit the people affected.

Had someone else been barking up this tree? Had others called in the name of paranormal study or with claims of abilities to help stop the antics of something intangible to science? Was the rumour of this haunting malicious, created for some malevolent reason perhaps during some personal feud? Or maybe, just maybe there was some substance to this. As compelled as I was to pursue this further, I had to respect the man's wishes. Dispirited, I closed the case and moved on.

With Pembrokeshire's rich tapestry of paranormal stories interwoven into the fabric of its history, I was soon busy again investigating and generally enjoying the subject in the beautiful county. But, like a seed starting to germinate, the house in Haverfordwest grew and grew in my mind. Soon it was eclipsing my everyday thought and haunting my dreams. I had cerebrally connected to the house in a way I could not understand. I was tempted to walk by it but rationale and resolve told me to stay away, to respect the people's wishes and not be discouraged by the failure to study the case in depth. I decided I r a break and booked a flight to Ireland to visit an old girlfriend.

After two days of relaxing and enjoying the Guinness, I checked my emails to discover rather unexpectedly, a message from the man from the house. My first presumption was that perhaps someone had told him I was still pursuing the case and that had agitated him. Surprisingly, he said that all involved had decided to talk to me about the house on the prerequisite that they were to remain anonymous and that the location of the house never be revealed. I was to take no photos inside or outside of the house and that arrangements would be made for me to speak to everyone involved so that concurrent and thorough documenting could take place. They hoped that it would be a cathartic experience and it may begin to make sense to them if explained to an outsider, particularly one with experience of the subject. They hoped there was an answer, I knew now that something was indeed happening in the house. I was delighted beyond belief but at the same time, there nagged a dark, foreboding about the house and it burrowed deep within my mind.

Two weeks later, the interviews had been completed and I have arranged these into a chronological order of events. The names of the people have obviously been changed along with any key information that may link the house and the people involved. Those I spoke to have nothing to gain from this recanting and there was genuine emotion and a sense of dread, fear and confusion and if what did happen there is true then this is truly one of the most disturbing and prolific hauntings investigated.

I shall leave you, the reader, to decide and draw your own conclusions.

***

John and Sarah are the principal witnesses to the events that occurred. I met John at a coffee shop by the River Cleddau in Haverfordwest for his interview over a period of two days. At a later date I met Sarah at her home a few miles away. All names in this transcript have been changed to protect the identity of the people involved. Neither currently live at the address. I also had the opportunity to speak to other relevant people who were witness to occurrences and events which have been included. I have edited the conversations into a more flowing fashion for the reader. Everyone involved has given me their consent for the publication of the events for which I am grateful. Here are the testimonials and I gladly extend the opportunity to the reader to decide for yourself, based on your own personal views and through the evidence presented to create your own theory on the case.

John: I met Sarah through work. It was one of those incidents that we both clicked straight away. This was about ten years ago, so I was in my late twenties and she was a little younger. Everyone would tease us about getting together but the timing was always wrong. She left and came back a year later and we both hit it off again and started dating.

Sarah: John was different back then, always laughing and joking, always kind and friendly and was always so confident. I liked him so much, I was very attracted to him, but I guess we didn't want to ruin a good thing but yeah...we got together eventually and it was great. It was a good time in my life. Wow, it seems so long ago now.

John: After a few months, we got a little flat together in the town centre a few minutes' walk from the shops. It was a nice time. We had no T.V, and would drink wine and chat and smoke and listen to music. The flat always seemed so bright and airy in hindsight. It sounds berserk now, but it was almost as if it was blessed.

Sarah: John loved that old flat so much; he could see the castle from the window. He loved popping down to the bakery to get fresh bread, or the paper or coming home with a few bottles of wine. People would visit all the time, it was nice as we were literally in the town centre so our friends and family would pop over on a Saturday on their way through town and we would have friends over in the evenings for supper. It felt good, it felt grown up, maybe a little pretentious with the music and wine and no T.V but at that time we were happy with each other and we didn't need anything else.

John: Not to say it was perfect as we did have rows as every couple does, couples who say they don't argue will one day have a huge row and that's when things go wrong, quickly. My advice is to not let things fester. It was a good time, I never wanted to leave but I guess we were heading towards thirty and it was a one bedroom flat and I think Sarah might have started thinking about family and settling down or just not paying rent and working and paying towards something that was ours but if there was a time machine then I would jump in it and travel back to August 1st 2003 and make sure that day played out differently. I will never forget that date, never, and I never wanted to leave. But a relationship is about two people not just one, you think that your doubts are just manifested through fear of the unknown, or because you don't like the idea of being tied down to a massive responsibility. It was never because I did not want to live and spend my whole life with Sarah, that was never the case.

Sarah: We were in work together and I was reading the local paper the *Western Telegraph* and I saw the house up for sale and I couldn't believe it, some friends of mine had lived there for a bit and I had stayed over after a night out. I remembered it being a cool place and I thought I'd love a place like this one day. It had so much character. So many houses have the same set-up, this was different. It was lovely.

John: I was sat in the office when Sarah came in with a great big smile and a copy of the paper under her arm. She showed me the house, a little black and white advert of a terraced house that I had walked past a million times and never even noticed. I have to admit that I didn't like it, I didn't want to go from the flat and rush into anything, I guess my lack of enthusiasm was painted on my face as her smile just vanished and she looked really hurt. I remember we had a huge bust up.

Sarah: We had a discussion on the future and where we were going, I could not believe why he wasn't more excited. Even to just go and look at it. I knew if He just looked at it then he would love it.

John: Sarah was furious when I said that we should have some kind of pre-nuptial. I think we had been together close to a year and surely that's not long enough. I laugh now but I had seen so many of my friends and family lose homes and end up with nothing. That sounds terrible right? It's like I was thinking the worse before it even happened but realistically everyone likes to think it through...yeah? Anyway I felt bad about it and told her to book us a viewing. As I said, if I could travel back in time I would have said no. I know we would have been at odds, maybe even had a huge falling out but we would have worked through it. I loved her so much. She was so beautiful and smart and I think that love was what made me say yes to view the house. What was the worst that could happen right?

Sarah: I did feel a little selfish but I knew it would be for the best and we were paying something near £350 to £400 a month for a small town flat plus bills on top of that. Also we could have no pets apart from a hamster, there was no garden and guests had to sleep on a bed settee in the living room, plus we were only a little bit further away. It was no difference in the time it took us to get to work or to go to the shops. John sulked for a bit but men do have a tendency to do that anyway when they don't get their way. I felt that we were basically wasting money renting and at the time, it felt right for us to take that next big step, to commit to each other and really start thinking about our future. It feels so strange saying that now.

John: To be honest, I didn't know much about buying a house, all I knew was that it was hard work and took a long time, in my mind we would view it and not be able to afford it or someone else would gazump it. Gazump, that is a word right? The house was valued at something crazy like £125K and I thought on our wages combined we could not afford that. But Sarah was the smart one, always was and always will be, she had done her research and even before the viewing of the house, in her mind it was ours. She came in on the 1st to tell me and the viewing was on the 3rd! I was livid, I was hoping it would take longer. So off we went from work one evening, to see this place.

Sarah: I remember being so excited and it was a beautiful evening and the sun was shining. We got to the house and I squeezed Johns hand so hard. I knew, I just knew he would love it. I had had a call from the estate agent a few hours before to say that they couldn't make it, but the woman who owned the house was happy to show us around.

John: It looked nothing special on the outside, there are a hundred or more houses in Haverfordwest that look the same. It was quite near a main road and I liked the fact that our flat was down a little lane out of the way but still in the centre of town. Sarah knocked on the front door, and this woman, sullen and joyless, probably a bit older than us answered. She didn't seem that excited that we were there. In my mind she would have been baking bread, tidying and arranging flowers around the house to make it more homely. In hindsight I bet she thought we were just another dumb young couple, looking to play grown-ups and there was no way she was going to get us to buy so she could get out of the house with a profit. It was like she was just going through the motions. She made absolutely no effort in her appearance or making the house look nice and tidy. I'm not a snob but seriously? Make an effort. Also it always seemed a bit weird that even the estate agent didn't turn up. I just thought they were probably enjoying a pint in a beer garden somewhere like maybe we should have been doing. At the time you don't notice things like that but I just thought the woman who owned the house was a bit of a weirdo.

Sarah: I have to admit the woman who owned the house didn't give us much of a welcome. It was like we were a nuisance. We went in and she said "*this is the living room, dining area over there; kitchen and bathroom back there and have a look upstairs*". She explained the layout in about a minute and said to look around if we wanted. It was like the life had been sucked out of her. I thought maybe she worked nights or something.

John: I thought wow! She's selling this so well, this woman should be on "The Apprentice". This was a £125k investment to us, not a second hand lawn mower. Her lack of enthusiasm made me want to just walk out.

Sarah: It was easy to sense that John was upset by the woman but thankfully, I had been in the house before and I knew where everything was so I conducted the tour of the house.

John: She hadn't even tidied up but I I'll admit, with the sun shining through the window, I was surprised by how long the house was in terms of it looked tiny on the outside and stretched way back. I could see why Sarah liked it, it was like a TARDIS. However, that woman's attitude really pissed me off.

Sarah: I took John up the stairs to show him the three bedrooms.

John: The advert said three bedrooms, there were in fact two. There was a master bedroom, a strange shaped attic conversion and a box room so small that a cat would get claustrophobic.

Sarah: I didn't know that there was a child living with the woman and when we went up to the attic conversion she was lying on the wooden floor colouring in some pictures she'd drawn. She was only about seven and the first thing she asked was *"Are you going to buy this so we can find a new home?"*

John: What a strange question then it clicked, the mum had put the kid up to it as emotional blackmail! In hindsight I wish I had paid more attention to what the girl was drawing as it was probably of me chained to bed, with my head spinning and spewing pea soup or something. It was such a weird set up, you don't prepare for these things but seriously, it was such a strange evening.

Sarah: I asked the woman what came with the house and she said the carpets and the kitchen furnishings. I asked her how low would she go in terms of the offer for the house and she said £105K. I was shocked as it was advertised at £125K and she was happy to drop twenty thousand pounds. She quickly added that was what she had paid for it.

John: I immediately thought what was wrong with it? This was in good economic times, not like now with the credit crunch and there was me thinking that someone would outbid us, or we would not be able to afford it and now the woman was desperate to get what she paid for it, not what it was valued as. Was there subsidence or damp or bad neighbours? There had to be something, but it seemed that woman and her kid just wanted to get out of there. I thought that maybe her and her husband had split up and she just wanted out. I don't think she was from around here. There are a lot of people down here in Pembrokeshire because of the military bases or oil refineries in the area.

Sarah: I took John into the garden, a lovely long garden with a shed at the end. We stood on the decking, I knew John would love the decking and I just blurted, *"Let's do this. Let's go for it"*. We could afford it on our wages, it was a bargain and it had a garden and spare rooms and it wouldn't work out much more than what we were paying for at the flat.

John: I admit that the place seemed really nice, I won't exaggerate and say that I sensed there was something wrong or that there was a feeling of foreboding. There was nothing like that at all, just a nice house. I said to Sarah that we need to think about it, need to talk first and work it out. I remember Sarah beaming like a kid who has been told they can have a present if they are good. As I said Sarah was smart and if we went for this then she would work out how we could do it. It was nice there on the decking with the sun shining. I love the summer and I can't abide the winter and I started imagining us living there, making plans for the decking, like we already lived there. That's always a mistake when you move in, imagining and creating in your mind. On the walk home Sarah was quiet; she was always quiet when she was computing in her mind. She was processing and organising everything that needed to be done; It's an amazing skill to have.

Sarah: John left everything to me, which was for the best. He of course came with me to the mortgage advisor and to the bank and to the estate agents. We put in an offer of £105K and it was accepted straight away. I was so anxious that it would all go wrong and we would lose it but on September 6th 2003 we had the keys. It happened so fast, it was incredible.

John: You have to give all the credit to Sarah, she worked so hard to make sure everything was in order. I was of course sad to leave the flat but once you started boxing things up and changing your details for the post then you kind of disconnect, and look forward to the new place. I was excited, I just wanted to click my fingers and be there in the new house with all the furniture in place. Plus we could have SKY TV at our new place which was exciting and Sarah started talking about kittens and puppies.

Sarah: John was like a kid that we would have SKY TV and the night before we were to have friends and family help us move in, he went over and cleaned the empty house from top to bottom, everything!

John: I actually spent the first night there on my own, cleaning, tidying, and organising. My Dad popped over with a bag of cleaning stuff and I showed him around. He loved the place, the house seemed much bigger as it was empty of furniture and clutter from the woman and her daughter. You came in through the front door into a tiny little hallway and then a door led you into the living room. In front of you was a big old fireplace with a window to your right. Off from the living room was a dining area with two doors and under the stairs was a little alcove. One set of double doors took you to the kitchen and through patio doors to the decking area and garden. The other door led to the bathroom. The stairs had no railing and had a small landing. The doors up here were thick and heavy with black latches, quite old fashioned but I liked them. One door opened to a small room which overlooked the street, another door to the main bedroom and finally the third to an attic conversion which was a low ceilinged room with wooden floors. You couldn't stand straight but it was long and quite wide and this part of the house due to its design was not attached to any of the other houses. Immediately I thought DEN! I could play music and not annoy the neighbours, drink wine, and play video games in this room. Sarah had designs on it to be a spare room, but we did compromise. The room was weird like some do it yourself enthusiast had gone mad with little cupboards, nooks and crannies. There was a door to the boiler at one end and a little door as you came in that ran the length of the room and was filled with Christmas trees and decorations from previous occupiers. I have to say that I felt nothing untoward that night. I had the radio on and I thoroughly cleaned the place and scrubbed the decking too. Dawn came and the sun shone through the one window at the front of the house and I loved the place, Sarah was right. It was a good place at that time.

Sarah: We didn't have much to move and some good friends and family got vans to help us, it was fun, the bed belonged to the flat and we had a few bits and bobs but not a huge amount. Family gave us a dining table and we bought a fridge and found a second hand washing machine that was advertised in the paper. We didn't even have a bed but John said don't worry we will sleep in sleeping bags till it arrives and have fish and chips for our first official night. Both of us were eager to get unpacked. We just had to wait for a proper sofa and for the bed to be delivered.

John: First night was kind of romantic, snuggled up on the bedroom floor in our sleeping bags, big grins, madly in love. We had work the next day and I slept fine, not a peep in the night.

Sarah: First night was absolutely fine. My alarm goes off at 7 on the dot and Johns literally a few seconds later. So I'm lying on the floor when my alarm goes off and then Johns; he shuts it off and the door to the bedroom just opened. It swung open. I could have sworn it was on a latch and the carpet was thick so you had to push it. John laughed and said *"Ok, Ok, we're getting up"* like the house wanted us up.

John: The bedroom door opened on the first morning, just swung open, I said something like *"Someone's fed up with us after just one night".* I thought I heard the latch lift but I won't swear to that.

Sarah: To be honest I didn't think much about it after as we had to go to work, everyone was excited about our move plus we still had lots to do with deliveries and unpacking. I had a lot of planning to do and of course a day's work too.

John: The door opening, I love stuff like that; well I used to love stuff like that. When I used to live back at my fathers I liked the all the shows about ghosts and I loved the X-files and I loved it when on Christmas Day the family got together, someone would always have a ghost story. I do remember with the door that it opened a little bit a first, like someone was peeping through and then it opened fully even on the thick carpet. In my mind it was like when I was little and my Gran or Dad would open the door a little to see if I was still asleep and when they saw me waking they would come on in. I miss my gran very much.

Sarah: I feel bad about this as I gave John hell but I used to keep all the important documents for the house in a file in a draw. You know, all the mortgage details, bills and so on and I kept everything organised. He didn't have to do much but sign where he had to sign. One day John and his mate were moving this big old heavy leather sofa, very old fashioned that we had bought from a second hand furniture shop and I needed to send off a document and I couldn't find it in the draw. I checked where I thought it could be and thought it's definitely in the house as I had it here yesterday. John is struggling to get the sofa in and I ask him where it is and he said he didn't know. I said he must, as I didn't have it and it had been in the top draw. John and his mate get the sofa in and he's sweating and flustered and says *"have you checked the top draw?"* of course I bloody had and we had a row. It was the first time we had rowed in front of a friend before. He swore on his life that he had not touched them. We calmed down and I keep looking, I can't find them and have to go through all the hassle of getting them re-done, so I got on my mobile and rang whomever it was I needed to get it sorted with.

John: She was adamant that I hid them from her, why would I do that? I like a prank as much as anyone but not with important stuff but I never doubted her, she was that organised, but moving house is stressful and maybe she had just forgotten where she had put them. I wasn't cross with her, it was just the settee weighed a ton and it was a nightmare to get into the house and a joke that maybe the hamster had them did not help at all.

Sarah: I was so upset that they had gone missing but John said he would help me look and we would find them. To make matters worse a few hours I decided I did not like where the settee was placed as I wanted it under the window. John and I pulled it across the room and John was staring at the floor. He looked so confused and there they were, the documents had been under the sofa. John swore they were not there when he put it down and I thought I would never leave something so important lying on the carpet with the front door wide open while they were getting the sofa in.

John: I couldn't explain it at all; I honestly did not see them when we brought in the settee and maybe I wasn't paying attention. My mate who was helping said he didn't see anything but as I said maybe we just didn't pay any attention. Sarah went very quiet as either she doubted herself or she blamed me, it was a strange afternoon.

Sarah: We soon forgot and got on with making the house a home. I was looking in the paper one night and some kittens were free to a good home and it was only a few minutes' walk away. I told John and he was happy enough and we went and got a kitten.

John: I love animals but that Kitten hated me, I got on better with the hamster. I even bought it a big climbing tree which it only used when I wasn't there! Anyway, I was sitting on the settee watching a DVD; we had a TV set but no SKY or anything yet, I think I was catching up on the series "24". The kitchen doors are open and it's dark back there and I thought I heard a noise and presumed it was the kitten or the fridge making a noise. As I looked away I thought I saw like a little surge of energy, a small ball of electricity. It was only for a second. I walked through the dining area into the kitchen; I didn't feel nervous or anxious, I thought maybe the cooker was playing up or it was a light from outside reflecting back in. The cooker was off and I went out the back on the decking and there was nothing unusual. I went back to the settee and it happened again. Now, I was worried as I suffer with migraine with what's called an aura, it's very common and they impair me so much that I have missed work and get togethers with friends and family as I'm useless when they strike. I can't see, I can't talk, and I have numbness in my arm and then have a cracking headache over my eye. I'm not afraid to admit but sometimes the pain is so severe that I've cried. One of the symptoms I have affectionately called the worm, it's a light that impairs my vision, like a blue worm across my vision which makes it difficult to focus. It's the first symptom and I thought *"Oh no, not a migraine!"* No migraine came so I just shrugged it off and never mentioned it to Sarah.

Sarah: One night I came out of the Bathroom after a shower and John was taking pictures of the kitchen in the dark. I thought he'd gone mad and he said that he thought the kitten was playing on its climbing tree in the kitchen and he wanted a photo. The kitten was upstairs sleeping on our bed. I just thought it was John being John. You know, he was kind of kooky.

John: A few nights later I saw the little light again, and this time I ran and got our camera and took a few pictures. I got them developed a few days later and there was nothing to see just the flash on the patio doors and the kitchen and the cats climbing tree. Sarah must have thought I'd had some kind of breakdown.

Sarah: I didn't feel that anything strange was happening and we started settling into a nice routine. We would finish work and John would have a bottle of wine open or a pot of green tea and we had a TV now. We'd snuggle up on the sofa I'd have the kitten all cwtched (snuggled up) up with me and we had just got into "24", the TV series.

John: We'd settle down for the evening and watch DVD's and I remember so vividly seeing something out of the corner of my eye towards the kitchen. We had this cream carpet and the light from the TV made everything look brighter but around the kitchen and bathroom area was shadowy. I was very aware of something moving, at first I just thought it was the flickering of the TV casting shadows, playing with my mind. This blur would disappear into the shadows and be gone but every night it came back. I could only see it from the corner of my eye and couldn't focus on it directly. At one stage I was so sure that I saw it that I got up to look, Sarah asked what was I doing and I said I thought I had seen a rodent, a rat or something moving by the kitchen. That is how convinced I was. This happened for a week and I did not utter a word to Sarah after I said I thought I saw a rat as I didn't want to upset her after everything with the bedroom door opening, the documents moving and the lights in the kitchen. Then one night this shadow, this blur moves up to the armchair we had across the room and it just stood there for a minute and disappeared back into the shadows. As I'm telling you now it has my hairs standing on end. It was a few feet tall and it seemed as if each day it got braver or stronger and got closer and closer. The night I knew something was happening and I hadn't gone mad was when it made its way in front of the TV and Sarah grabbed my arm.

Sarah: I had seen it for days, slowly moving by the kitchen and disappearing in the shadows. It was small, maybe 2 feet tall, it had no real form just something in the corner of the eye and the night it stood in front of the TV you could see it, a strange black blur, it is so strange to describe, you would have to see it to understand. I squeezed John's arms so hard it bruised and when the TV went black for a second and the thing was gone. That was the last time we saw the blur, it was moving around the room at floor level for around two weeks every night and then it made itself known and we never saw it again.

John: Sarah and I were really calm about it, we were of course a little frightened but as far as I knew we had a ghost. It was as simple as that. You hear so many stories of hauntings and pretty much everyone I know has a story about a ghost or a UFO What can you do, call the police? Get a priest? This thing did not seem bad, I did not get a sense of dread, and it just spooked me. I thought it was cool at the time, maybe get some evidence, get a picture and make a fortune but we decided not to tell anyone as people would be coming over to stay and visit and we did not want to upset them. I thought I'm not going to lose any sleep over it. It's mad to think that things got so bad that I began to dread the night, but I'm getting ahead of myself.

Sarah: I was upset, really upset. I didn't want to believe in such things, I told myself that there had to be an explanation. John loved it, I knew he did, but I hated it. My first thought was that maybe there was carbon monoxide in the room or something that was causing us to hallucinate. It was always at the same time of night, around 10pm, and both of us had seen it. John got mad when I made us watch TV with the light on. I asked my dad to come over and he put in a brand new carbon monoxide detector and checked the boiler and everything. He said it was fine but I still got the gas man to check, he said everything was in good working order. John started staying up later after I went to bed to watch DVD's but I knew he was down there with his camera trying to get a photo. I just wanted him to come to bed and snuggle, not be a ghost buster. I was terrified on my own.

John: I have to say that it did excite me to the extent that if we could record evidence that we could be rich and famous! I know it sounds stupid now, but that's what I thought. It was my very own x-file! I was like the people on "Most Haunted". Sarah thought it might be the boiler, or radon gas seeping through the floor plus there was all this fuss about this new mobile phone technology that was going to be used in the area; leaflets came through the door saying that it needs to be stopped, petitions need to be signed and protests attended as the technology was based on cold war weapons, made people depressed and ill and could even cause diarrhoea. Berserk I know, but it's a theory and who knows maybe it was responsible. The house was quiet too; the walls were so thick that you never heard the neighbours to either side of us, no TV; there were no arguments heard and not even a headboard banging in the night. The Walls were stone and probably a few feet thick.

Sarah: Nothing seemed to happen for a few weeks and the nights began to draw in and the house seemed warm and comfortable and John, the kitten and the hamster all seemed settled. John hates the winter as he suffers from a seasonal disorder that makes him prone to depression. I didn't fully appreciate at the time what it is, but it's awful to see someone so bright and cheerful become more and more down and sorrowful but he would always try and fight it. Well, he did but I guess he just got worn down by everything that started to happen.

John: The cat and I started to get on a bit and it would chill out more and sit by me on the settee. The hamster would roll about in its big plastic ball on the carpet and they both got on well. One evening I walked from the kitchen into the dining room and there on the settee the cat was hissing at something, its ears back and tail snaking around. I thought what's up? I said *"Lucky"*, Lucky was the cats name and it just growled this insane growl and I walked towards the settee and it was like I had walked into something absolutely freezing. We had radiators on and we had been cooking and Sarah had been in the bath so the house was warm and cosy. I could literally map the area of the coldness with my hand, it was about four feet tall and maybe a foot across and from the top to the carpet it was freezing. Then in a second it was back to normal temperature and the cat just scarpered upstairs. I have since read about cold spots but it was like there was something there, just stood there, staring at the cat and the cat could see it, sense it, I don't know how to describe it but the cat was certainly aware of it.

Sarah: John told me about Lucky; but animals, particularly cats, always have a tendency to do that weird hissing and staring at the wall thing. I just thought the cold spot was a draft or maybe something to do with the fireplace, it was blocked up but maybe a brick had come loose. I wasn't there so I can't give any more information on that.

John: About this time we finally had our SKY installed. I was thrilled we could finally catch up on so much TV that we'd missed. The guy who installed it I knew well as a friend of mine had married his sister and he set the TV all up and showed me how it all worked; you couldn't fault the service. Sarah and I were excited and she'd just had her bath and we settled down and at 10pm it just went off. I was cross as you would expect, as we were excited. Next day I call SKY, they said there was no fault but they would try something or other. I get home from work and it's working fine. 10pm it goes off, I'm decidedly pissed off. So Sarah calls SKY in the morning and they say there is no detectable fault from there but there was obviously a problem and they would send out an engineer. The same guy who set it up comes over and again. He's great, he puts in a new box, does a load of tests, and checks the signal and all's fine. That night at 10pm off it goes. Three new boxes and a new dish later the problem is finally solved. We were told that they could not understand what was happening that the signal and the equipment were working fine. I have had SKY before and after and never experienced anything like that. You start to think, 'was that just a genuine fault or was something messing with us'.

Sarah: The Problem with the satellite dish was so strange and the poor people on the phone and the engineer must have thought we were nutters because they couldn't find a problem. It did cause stress between us because at one time John just gave up and went straight to bed after we finished work. His SAD (seasonal affective disorder) was starting to kick in and he just wanted to relax and enjoy our evenings together. I went up to see him; he said to just leave him alone. He was never usually like that. It's sad to see someone with so much energy just lying there looking lifeless and miserable but he would drink and that never made it better, so maybe he was to blame for it to begin with.

John: I do get down but I always try and buck up. I remember one night I made a terrible mistake of getting hammered on a bottle of red. In the night I had to get up to use the toilet which was downstairs. I always tried to be quiet as I didn't want to wake Sarah; plus we had started to lock the kitten in the kitchen with its bed, litter tray and climbing frame. The Kitchen doors would not close tight so we rested a dining chair against the doors to stop lucky from escaping and running around the house. The hamster was normally up at night doing hamster things in its cage but you get used to it. I put on the landing light which was enough for me to see down the stairs and the bathroom door. I tip toed down and went in the bathroom and turned on the bathroom light and went to the loo. I was stood there and this overwhelming coldness overtook me, all the hairs stood up on my neck and on my arms and I swear I felt a breath on my neck. It was as if someone was stood right up close behind me. I was petrified, absolutely terrified and I spun around expecting to see Sarah, to see something; nothing was there. I dashed off up the stairs and hid in bed with the landing light still on. That was the first of many times that would happen to me.

Sarah: Yeah, it happened to me lots. A few times when I got out of the shower I felt something there, just watching. Sometimes I would feel this deep coldness cover me, I know you're going to be cold when you get out of the shower but this was freezing cold. I would be sat on the loo and I could see my breath, that's how cold it would get; it was really unnatural. It got to the stage where I would try and be as quick as possible to have a shower or use the loo so as not to spend too much time in there. It was not a good feeling at all; I always felt a sense of menace.

John: There were times that I'd have a bath and Sarah a shower or vice versa at the same time as we did not like being in there alone at night. I can't recall very much happening in the day time just mainly at night. This sounds very odd and people will think me mad, but I always, always got the sense it was a woman. I can't explain why I feel that, there was no perfume smell or anything to determine what it was, but from that first night, I always thought it was a woman.

Sarah: Funny that John would say that but I always sensed it was a man. It's strange how the imagination works but I imagined this creepy, leering man just lurking in there like some weirdo sex pest. We of course had double glazed frosted glass with a curtain in there and there was a radiator that was quite often on airing our underwear or a towel. It was an awful thing to experience, you can't do anything. I cried one day, just by considering having a shower as the feeling was so intense and so awful in there. People have no idea just how suffocating and harsh the atmosphere was in there. It was like a cold, sickly tension. But then, suddenly, it stopped for a bit, just long enough for us to think things were going to get back to normal. The house had a habit of doing that, it would do things and stop, just for a short time and then it would do something new or something more intense.

John: All of this had taken place over about seven or eight weeks because it really stepped it up a gear around the time the fair came to town, up in Portfield by the rifleman's field, which is normally end of October, perhaps the start of November. When Sarah's twin nephews came to stay the weekend, we were to take them to the fair and they were going to see the kitten and our new place.

Sarah: I made John swear on his life that he wouldn't say anything or try and frighten the boys but you could see in his eyes that the spark of excitement about the strange events had gone. It was no longer a ghost hunting adventure to him; this was real and it was tiring and depressing. He looked drained and tired and the winter was starting to entrench. He was drinking more, like he was just trying to knock himself out before bed and just get to the morning. I couldn't sleep, I'd hear the hamster in his cage but now and again I thought I heard the bathroom door open and hear the stairs creaking. With everything going on, my imagination was running wild.

John: You know things have gone south when you're practically running to work in the morning to get some peace.

Sarah: My nephews, Eric and Sam were coming over after school on the Friday. They were ten then and they were excited as we were going to the fair. John got on well with them both and we were both looking forward to having them over. I'd had this nagging feeling though about what if the house played up when they were here? What if they got scared or frightened? John thought that if they slept in the den then they should be ok as it was a new part of the house, an extension. Nothing seemed to happen in there are far as we knew, in fact John spent more time in there, watching DVD's and drinking wine. I felt like I was losing him.

John: I admit that the house was depressing me; the excitement was replaced with dread. I spoke to a few close friends about it and they suggested that we get the house blessed or call in a priest. Just sounds crazy now, something that science cannot prove exists affecting us so badly. I know this sounds stupid but I hated having a pee or going to the loo or having a shower because it was like there was something there, something wrong or sinister just watching.

Sarah: It practically ended any physicality between us, you know of an intimate nature. How could you be naked or physical while at the back of your mind you're anxious that something is watching or that something will open the door? Now and again we would stay at friends and make up for it then, it was like a huge weight was lifted off our shoulders and it was new and like when we were together for the first time but then we would also have this dread that we would have to go back to the house. What would be waiting for us? No home should ever feel like that.

John: It was good having Eric and Sam over and it brightened the place up. They loved the cat and the hamster and quickly made themselves at home. They loved playing on the PlayStation.

Sarah: We took them to the fair and it was nice to be out. I love the fair; the sounds of the generators, the smell of the candy floss and hot dogs and the boys were running around and John and I were trying to keep up. There was this really, really old fashioned ghost train, well not so much as a ghost train but you walked in and went through some creepy rooms. I went in first with Sam and then John went in with Eric. Something happened because Eric came out on his own and said that John couldn't move.

John: I went in with one of the boys and it was a shitty ride that cost me £8 for four entries, just little rooms with lots of corners to walk around and mirrors and string hanging down so it felt like someone was touching your hair. Sam, no it was Eric, Eric thought it was rubbish, and darted off and came back saying it was dull and nothing happened. I kept expecting a man in a mask to dive out and frighten us. I got about half way and there was a small room with a flashing light and I just freaked. I felt so despondent and low, like really depressed. I just felt like a statue, it sounds silly but I just wanted to be a kid again with my Dad and Gran. Life was so much easier then; back then, all this weird ghost crap was just stories and now it was real and in the home with me and the woman I loved. Maybe it was the nostalgia, memories of going to the fair with my father or the cold and dark of the winter but I just had this mammoth feeling of despair.

Sarah: I had to go back on and spend another couple of pound and get him out. He looked like he had been crying but he came out and smiled and joked for the boys. He never let on but I felt like I had lost him that night. I felt like he regretted buying the house, that I had ruined him, ruined us. It was not my fault what was happening at the house. As we were mulling around the fair I met my friend who had owned the house prior, the time when I stayed over after a night out. Eric and Sam were on the bumper cars and John and I had been waiting for them. We exchanged hugs and pleasantries and John bluntly blurted *"Is the house haunted?"* My friend paused and almost regretfully said it was. Her ex-partner who had lived there had had a rough time. She said that she was working nights and it got so bad that her boyfriend would sleep at his mum's house as he hated being there on his own.

John: Inside I was cross that her friend had never warned Sarah, but Sarah would not have listened anyway. Sarah was stubborn and besides who the fuck is going to believe that actual ghosts mess with people and haunt an actual house? I'm sorry for the language but it still frustrates me to this day. Anyway, She told us that her boyfriend, husband whoever he was, had seen things come down the stairs when he was sat watching TV, she claimed that it would walk around downstairs moving things, making noises, running up the stairs while he lay in bed terrified. It got to the stage that he had to go to his mum's just to sleep. I felt sick, I felt angry.

Sarah: She told us that one night her boyfriend called her, pleading for her to finish work early as he was frightened, things had been happening in the house. She claimed she never saw anything; but that you knew there was something not right there. As she worked nights and was out on the weekends she didn't have much involvement especially at night when the occurrence seemed stronger and more prolonged. I knew that their relationship ended suddenly and they sold up. Eric and Sam came off the ride and we quickly changed the subject.

John: We got home and I got straight on the wine, I was shaking. I kept getting chills up and down my spine and I knew that I was just freaking myself out. Every noise had to be a ghost, every creak was a ghost; I was losing it, I felt that it was pushing us out, constantly pushing our buttons. It was winning.

Sarah: I put the boys to bed and they were exhausted. I went down stairs and sat at the dining table was John with a massive glass of red wine. I sat by him and I told him off, I told him he had to get a grip that whatever was happening had a rational explanation and the house was ours. Ours! I said that his SAD and his drinking were making him depressed and susceptible to anxiety and fear and that we needed to be strong, to fight for our home by ignoring anything that was happening, to push back and be happy and embrace that happiness.

John: Sarah gave me a pep talk and you know what? She was right. At first I resisted all hope and then I realized she was right. Maybe what was happening had an explanation and if it didn't, then push it out the way? We were alive and it was OUR home. A home that hopefully one day we would have children of our own and a life. I have to say that I felt better. We went to bed together that night and for the first time in a long time we snuggled and we slept well. It makes me sad now thinking of how happy we were for that brief time, it might have been the last time we were truly happy and in love.

Sarah: I woke up and the sun was streaming through the sky light and John was stretched out across the bed like a starfish and deep in sleep. I heard something shuffling around on the landing and the latch went on the door and it opened a little but this time it was Sam. He looked tired and upset. I sat up and said was he O.K and he said that someone has been in the Den with them opening the cupboard doors and running around. He said it wasn't very funny of John to play tricks like that.

John: I was so confused, I had slept all night. I slept in the inside of the bed against the wall as Sarah would get up first to use the bathroom. Sarah looked at me and she knew I hadn't moved but what do you say to the kid. *"It's Ok son, it was a ghost"* or *"Yeah it was me sneaking around in a room with two ten year old boys sleeping in it"* either way it was going to portray me in a very poor light. I was furious, I knew what it was.

Sarah: I told Sam that it was probably the pipes or the neighbours in another house. I had no idea what to say so I just lied to him.

I was fortunate enough to have a telephone conversation with Sam (real name changed to protect identity) who, now 20 years old, had the opportunity to speak to his aunty Sarah about the night in question when he was much older. Eric his twin brother was unavailable for comment as he was currently working overseas. This is Sam's account and perspective on the events of that night:

Sam: What a strange night, I never really believed in ghosts and aliens but that night still gives me the shivers even now. I was only ten or eleven but I remember the night. Sarah and John had just bought this new house and they had got a cat and it was around the time the fair was in town. We enjoyed seeing them as they were always fun and treated us like grown-ups and gave us more freedom to relax. We went to the fair and had a great time, I felt a little ill from the hotdogs and sweet stuff but apart from that it was fun. They had this strange attic conversion, a weird shape, low ceiling and everything made of wood. There was a fold out bed in there and Eric and I shared it, It was cool in there as John had a PlayStation 2. We played some fighting game until Sarah popped her head in and said *"time to sleep boys"*. She left the landing light on, so light was coming in from under the door so you could make out the shape of the room and we knew where to head to if we needed to get up in the night. At the far end of the room was a small door which was access to the boiler. You could hear the boiler doing its thing when John and Sarah were using the water or something downstairs. I didn't feel uncomfortable at all, just tired and excited as in the morning we were all going to go into town for breakfast. I woke up and had no idea what time it was but the den was pitch black and no light was coming in under the door. I heard no boiler or anything but I heard what sounded like a door slowly opening. The sound wasn't coming from the direction of the main door, but the little boiler door at the other end of the den. Eric was fast asleep and breathing deeply. It sounded like the door opened and closed a few times, like it was opened as far as it could and then slowly closed again and then opened and so on, a few times. I was scared, I remember holding my breath trying to listen and then I heard what sounded like something run across the den, like tiny feet, not like an animal but like the way a child or toddler would. I was terrified but I was too scared to scream or shout. The footsteps ran straight past the fold out bed and I heard what sounded like the whoosh, whoosh of material and then the boiler room door closed, not loudly with a bang but with more force than when I first heard it and it clicked as it closed shut. Eric said he heard nothing or saw anything and I must have dreamt it but I don't believe I did and it scared me. I hoped it was John playing a prank but Sarah told me in the morning that it was pipes under the floorboards, making it sound like someone was walking about and I believed her. It wasn't until a few years ago that she told me what had happened in the house. I think we were lucky, as scary as it was, some of the stuff that happened would have put me in a mental hospital if I'd been there. I never stayed there again. I feel sorry for John, he was good to us and that was one of the last times we saw him. That house did, in my opinion, ruin them both; people can say it was a dream or I made it up but it was real and frightening.

Sarah: When Sam was about 16, I had a chat with him about the house, the pressures it put on me and John. Sam was adamant that there was something in the room that night. Nothing could fit in the boiler cupboard as it was obviously filled with the boiler, you could say it was the wind or the pipes or even an animal on the roof or guttering; but I know, that it was whatever inhabited the house with us. John initially joked in the early days that he didn't mind having a ghost as long as it helped towards the bills and he would blame odd socks on it but by this stage it felt like we were being forced out, that we were the intruders.

John: After the night with the boys in the room I decided that I had to find out why this was happening. It wasn't a case of imagination or creaking old floor boards or the wind, there was something definite happening in the house. Not only had Sarah and I witnessed the activity, but it was of course, affecting us, traumatising us. Now it was Sam who'd had an experience when he stayed over. Sarah's friend who had lived here had said that there was something not right with the place; I was beginning to feel like her ex must have. I took it upon myself to conduct some proper investigation. I even agreed to have the house blessed.

Sarah: Some friends of ours were into spiritual and holistic practice and they seemed very grounded and knowledgeable about spirituality and life after death. I spoke to one of them and they referred us to this middle aged woman with a really nice demeanour, she was relaxed and said not to worry as she has experienced such things before and all the house needed was to be blessed and the spirits as she called them would find peace and leave and it would be like our home was new and more importantly it would be ours again.

John: I started investigating where we lived and what used to be there before us but there was nothing of consequence that could be linked to a haunting, you know like an old hospital or a burial ground. Haverfordwest is a very old town and maybe something had been there, nothing leapt out at me in the re-search, I needed to find something that I could connect the hauntings to. The house had been built over a hundred years ago and looking through the archives at the library I could not find anything about the address or the street. One very strange thing I discovered in the deeds was that seven different owners occupied that house since 1986. We moved there in 2003, so that's eight in less than twenty years. Maybe that was usual for the type of house and the worth and value of it, but my mind I just thought about how sullen and odd the woman was who showed us the house on the viewing. Had she like us and Sarah's friend experienced strange and unusual behaviour in the house? It all started to piece together like a jigsaw, the eight occupiers in seventeen years, Sarah's friend's ex-partner and the sullen woman and her kid. There was something very wrong happening here and it wasn't only us that it had happened to.

Sarah: The spiritualist woman came over to the house one Saturday when John and I were at home. As soon as she came through the door she said *"yes, yes, there is something here."* She smiled and said that we shouldn't worry and that the house still had occupants from the past that either didn't want to go, or didn't know they had passed on.

John: What the woman said just chilled me; I was still sceptical, as we had told our friends what was happening and they had told this woman. She had then had long discussions with Sarah on the situation. To be honest, it wasn't like she was there to see our new washing machine; she was there to help us get rid of the ghost or ghosts. She knew our predicament.

Sarah: It was a very relaxing experience. We sat in the living area and had a chat while drinking herbal tea; we talked about how it was affecting us as a couple and how what was supposed to be a good thing, buying and living in this house, for us was now a living nightmare. She spoke in depth that we had to emit an internal positive energy to push away the darkness and the sadness. She told us that our internal light would protect us from evil and be a beacon, to help the spirits pass into the spirit world and find happiness. She lit some incense sticks around the room and then asked us to follow her as she walked around with a lit incense stick, making sure the smoke and fragrance went into every corner and into every room. She spoke softly, reassuring the spirits that everything would be ok in the spirit realm if they just let go; that it was mine and Johns time in the house now and the house had to a happy place, not a sad place for the dead to linger in. She said that the den had a vortex that was generating energy for spirits to manifest and she told them that their loved ones who had passed were waiting for them in the afterlife. It was very emotional and I felt tingles on my scalp on down my neck and back. It was an amazing experience.

John: I expected the woman to say *"This house is cleansed"* like in the movie Poltergeist but I will admit I hung onto every word and I believed everything she said. I wanted a normal life together with Sarah and if this worked then great. I imagined that a bright orb of white light was in my chest pushing away the bad presence in the house.

Sarah: The woman left and John and I hugged and I started crying. I so wanted this to work; we needed this to work.

John: Immediately after the house had been blessed we felt bright and cheery and nothing seemed to happen. The walls didn't start bleeding and the settee didn't start flying around the room. We were cautious of course, and still very worried, but I still believed in my bright orb light inside me and that the spirits had got to go to heaven or where ever you go at the end. Then, it started again and this time it was more intense; It was much more frightening.

Sarah: I couldn't believe it; I just could not believe it. This time it felt like it was stronger, like it was angry that we dared try and evict it from its home. It was our home!

John: When it all started to kick off again I told Sarah to phone this spirit woman, but the woman said that she had tried and that the spirits obviously didn't want to go and to try and get an exorcist! I was furious but Sarah said that the lady had tried to help us for free and that we had to be positive and keep believing that the house was ours and hopefully the spirits would give up and we would win.

The lady in question who performed the blessing was unavailable for comment.

John: The next few days; after the blessing, just going to the toilet or for a shower was depressing as the intensity of the presence in there was overwhelming. People say it's the living not the dead we need to fear but the psychological suffering was beyond belief. This sounds insane but I made sure I went to the toilet as much as I could in work so I didn't have to go at home. My thoughts were severely dark, I thought about death most of the time. I know I suffer with depression but never like that before. It was like hope finally died.

Sarah: One night I was in bed, John was back on the wine big time and was passed out next to me, snoring. I lay there in the darkness thinking what had we done to deserve this and would things ever get better. I thought I heard a noise downstairs; I thought, please be the hamster running in its wheel or trying to gnaw its way through the cage again. So I'm lying there, trying to listen but John is snoring, so I try and nudge him so he turns on his side and he goes quiet for a bit and then unmistakably, I hear the bathroom door open and close again. I just kept thinking over and over *"please go away, please go away"*, then something ran up the stairs. In a few seconds, something made it up the stairs and onto the landing it was so quick and I could sense that it was on the other side of the door and I swear I heard the latch jiggle, and then I screamed.

John: I don't know what happened but Sarah was screaming. I woke up not knowing where I was or what was happening, I was still pissed. I jumped to the end of the bed and tumbled to the floor and Sarah turned on the light, she was sobbing uncontrollably. I asked what was happening and she said it was at the bedroom door. I tell you now, the last thing I wanted to do was to open that bloody door but I had to, just had to. So I pull up the latch slowly and pulled the door open. I expected to see a ghostly face or hell knows what and there was nothing. The landing was freezing cold and I was terrified. I thought let's just pack our things and be gone.

Sarah: When John opened the door I just expected to see something there. Like a ghastly skulled ghoul or something from a horror movie; there was nothing. John said perhaps with everything that was going on that maybe I'd just had a nightmare but I was wide awake, I didn't drop off or get any sleep that night. I swear that something opened the bathroom door, closed it and then ran up the stairs and tried to open our bedroom door.

John: I don't think people will fully understand the intensity of it all. We had been in the house maybe ten weeks, maybe three months tops and all of this is happening. We'd gone from things going missing, to cold spots, lights in the kitchen, blurry little figures in the living room, the presence in the bathroom, Sam being upset in the den and now something running around in the dark while we were in bed. What a terrible, terrible time.

Sarah: A night or two later and John and I are in the kitchen talking, we still had a life you know, work, family and friends. Some friends were down the following weekend and they were going to stay at ours, we were planning for that, but all the time you're thinking; *"should we tell them, should we actually tell them that all this weird shit is going to happen?"* But at the same time you feel selfish, you don't want to warn them as I needed them. I needed them to be in the house. John was drunk most evenings now and depressed and our relationship was not in a good state. We were both scared and maybe if some other adults were in the house maybe we would be safer, maybe nothing would happen or if they experienced something then maybe they would have a solution or an explanation. I just wanted them to stay so badly.

John: I remember we were in the kitchen chatting and making supper when we heard above us footsteps. Now the den ran the length of the Kitchen and above the bathroom and a little bit into the dining area. We hear these footsteps. They were heavy on the wood, not like a child as Sam heard but footsteps like ladies heels on the wooden floor and they walked the entire length of the den. We looked at the ceiling like we were watching it happen, following it with our eyes and whatever was making those sounds turned on its heel and walked back across to above us and then we heard the boiler room door slam.

Sarah: It was so scary but John did the strangest thing, he ran and grabbed his camera and sprinted up the stairs and barged into the den and shouted *"Come on you fucker, come on show yourself"* while taking pictures around the den. The fact he took control made me feel better but I just wish he hadn't baited it so much. We were to pay for that.

John: I guess I just lost the plot. I was sick and tired of its games. It had our attention and I wanted proof, hard proof that it existed so maybe I could take that evidence to someone who could help us or make us enough money so we could leave. I thought if this thing wants to frighten us then carry on and I'll catch it, I will get a photo or a recording and I would win, not it, but me. It was crazy to think that, but it's not like you have been burgled and you can fit better locks and get an alarm or a big dog. It's not like you're fighting a real person where you can kick or throw a fist or grab a baseball bat or scream for the police. How do you take on something that there is no proof that it even exists? But guess what it goes and does next?

Sarah: As soon as John comes back into the Kitchen the footsteps start again from above and he ran back upstairs and again nothing was there. It stopped as soon as he got to the top of the stairs. It was like it was playing with John or showing him who was boss. We got the photos developed the next day and there was absolutely nothing just the den illuminated by the flash. No ghostly apparition or orbs of light or strange shadowy figures. There was nothing.

John: I think it was the next night that was the worst night....it was horrible.

Sarah: What happened that night was terrifying, I don't expect people to believe what happened, and in fact I don't expect anyone to believe any of it, if you were not there or if you haven't experienced anything like it then how can you believe it?

John: We had gone to bed, I probably had been drinking, and I pretty much did every night. I dozed off and a huge crash woke me up. I thought maybe a car had crashed outside or someone had put a brick through the living room window.

Sarah: There was this smash, like a window being smashed in. I thought we were being burgled.

John: There was all this banging downstairs like the living room was being turned upside down, you could hear the draws being opened and slammed and you could hear rummaging. We were being burgled. All of this is happening so quickly and then it sounded like someone ran up the stairs and we both heard the bedroom door being pushed, we heard the metal of the latch and then silence.

Sarah: It was like a few men were searching for something down stairs, opening cupboards, doors and draws and then they came up the stairs and the door moved against the latch. I was paralysed with fear. You hear about robbers tying people up, hurting them...doing much worse things. John got the light on and was sat there bolt up with a mug in his hand like he was ready to throw it. I thought the police will be here on their way as someone must have heard the window smash and all the chaos downstairs. From the smash waking us up to the bedroom door being pushed took about thirty seconds. I was too frightened to even get up and dash across and get my mobile which was charging on the dresser across the room.

John: Even with everything that had been happening nothing had scared me more than this but you get these thoughts in your head like if there is someone in the house then I will hurt them. I will do what it takes to protect Sarah and us. I'm not a hard tough bloke who fights or anything but at that moment I thought if someone is in the house and I hurt them or worse, then I would happily go to prison than see either of us get hurt. I would imagine any man out there who hears this would do the same. There was silence for ages, not a sound and I had the lyrics of a song that I liked going around and around in my head, stuck in there like it was on repeat and it was from a band called *System of a down* and the lyrics were *"I'm sitting in my room, with a needle in my hand, just waiting for the tomb, of some old dying man."* People will laugh when they hear that, but I couldn't get those lyrics out of my head. Strange I know but I remember it so clearly, so vividly. I don't think it had any relevance to what was happening but it was just stuck in my mind.

Sarah: John whispered that it sounded like it was over, but I didn't hear anything go back down the stairs. I felt like something was still there on the landing maybe listening, trying to hear if we were awake or asleep. John started to get out of bed really slow with the mug in his hand, he was only in his boxers and he started to head for the dresser where our mobiles were. There were things like a brush, scissors, anything he could use as a weapon and then suddenly huge heavy footsteps ran down the stairs, then there was a huge crash and the slam of a door. It was awful.....absolutely awful.

John: I thought that whoever was on the landing saw that we had the light on; heard me moving about, thought that we had no doubt called the police and got out of there as quickly as possible.

Sarah: John made for the bedroom door, I screeched at him what if they were still in the house. He Pointed at the skylight and whispered that the sun was starting to come up. He grabbed the scissors from the dresser and tossed me my phone which was dead despite me having it on charge all night; I was so frustrated and frightened.

John: I slowly opened the door and fair dues to Sarah; she got out of bed and stood by me. I know it doesn't sound manly at all but I was glad she was with me. I slowly opened the door expecting a blacked gloved hand to grab me but I could see nothing in the gloom. I flicked on the landing light on and shouted as loud as I could *"POLICE ARE ON THE WAY, HAND ME THE CRICKET BAT AND CALL YOUR BROTHERS!"*

Sarah: John shouted down the stairs saying that the police were on the way and that we had weapons and people were on their way to help us. He did it so if there was anyone down there that hopefully they would panic and get out of there. We had nothing of worth, nothing of value just a TV and DVD player but nothing worth taking. You have to realize that we were pretty broke most of the time as we had to buy furniture and bits and bobs for the house; plus Christmas was around the corner and we never had much money in the house. Poor Lucky the cat was down there, I was worried he had escaped through an open door or smashed window or that they had stepped on him or done something terrible to him.

John: I was on the landing in only my pants and Sarah was holding onto my arm. I thought it had to be a smash and grab, there was only one window and door at the front of the house and near impossible to get in through the back garden. I didn't want to go down the stairs and I kept expecting to hear someone start shouting like the police or a neighbour to see if we were OK, I told Sarah to stay on the landing.

Sarah: John told me to stay, I didn't want to be alone but he said if someone was still downstairs then to run in the bedroom and try and get the dresser in front of the bedroom door and try and get out through the skylight. I don't think I could have reached it or even fit through, it was only small but I guess he was just trying to keep me safe.

John: I started going down the stairs, dawn had broken but it was gloomy down there and I was bricking it. I kept expecting to see a man down there or for a hand to grab my foot on the way down. The Bathroom door was wide open and the frosted window at the back was not smashed. As I came to the bottom of the stairs and into the dining area, I expected to see the window smashed behind the settee and the curtain billowing in the wind, but the window was fine. The Kitchen doors were still shut with a dining chair against them to stop Lucky from running around at night. I flicked on the dining room and kitchen light and there was no sign of a break in. I turned on the light in the living room and opened the door to the little hallway that led to the front door and the front door was intact, locked and chained from the inside. The front window had not been forced.

Sarah: I kept shouting *"John, are you OK?"* and *"John, what's happening?"* and he kept telling me to shush. Then he said to come down and that nothing had been broken into. He kept repeating *"I don't understand, I don't understand."*

John: I told Sarah that it was OK to come down, as I turned I saw that over by the armchair we had a wooden unit thing where we kept our CD player and Sarah had photos and things she collected on there; on the floor was about a dozen or so CD's and they had all been arranged into a spiral shape.

Sarah: When I saw the CD's all arranged into a spiral I just cried and sobbed and ran over and kicked them. John was mad saying we should have taken a picture as evidence. Evidence of what? Would people think that's definitely a ghost because it re-arranged the CD's? No, they would think us insane. I remember just lying on the floor, sobbing, I had experienced the worst night of my life. I wanted to leave and never come back.

John: I think it would have been easier if we had have been burgled as we could have dealt with that. We would have the police over and fitted better locks and thought ourselves grateful that we were not harmed, but how do you deal with this? I swear to you now, it sounded like something tore that house apart and something ran upstairs and was stood on the landing pressed against the bedroom door. It must have happened around 6am and from the time I woke up to getting downstairs took about five minutes, tops. It was no hallucination or bad dream, it was no prank and Sarah and I were together in bed when we heard it. We both heard it, we both experienced it. Sceptical people out there can think what they want and I can't blame them but something was in the house and it was mere feet from us behind the bedroom door. I held Sarah for ten, fifteen minutes while she sobbed and shook. She was in shock, we both were, and then she looked up and let out this massive wail.

Sarah: John was just holding me, telling me it would be ok. OK how? But he was trembling and he was crying too. I looked up at the Kitchen door and there on the chair that was pushed against the kitchen door was a framed picture of us both. It was just leant against the back of the chair, ʒ us. I hadn't put it there, it had been on the wall and I just screamed and screamed.

John: Whatever it was had sent us a powerful message. I just wanted to run out into the street and shout for help.

Sarah: You have no idea how it feels to be totally helpless. No one could help us. I knew we had to start to look for another place to live, but we had no money. Everything we had saved had gone into the house and our friends and family had no room for us. I know they would want us, but you can't just move a home into someone else's. What could we do, go down to the council office and say *"Can we have a new house please, ours is haunted?"*

John: I checked the rest of the house and there was definitely no sign of a break in. The windows were locked from the inside and the front door still had the chain on; so there was in my opinion, no way that someone had got into the house. Lucky was safe too. Sarah spoke to her Dad who came over and I spoke to my best friend who did not know what to say. I knew it was no good calling these so called ghost hunters, no offence meant, or a physic medium. The woman who blessed the house had made it worse. We had to move out but it's not like you can just get up and leave that instant. We needed to sell up or find someone to move in and rent it and we needed money for temporary living. We both went to work that day and it was one of the longest days of my life.

Sarah: I just didn't want to go back at all, but on the way home John said that yes we needed to move out but it would take time. Even though we were both scared out of our wits, apart from psychologically and emotionally neither of us had been harmed. He said lets acknowledge it, treat it like a family member. I thought; *"He's lost the plot now."*

John: I just thought lets be nice to it, it wants attention. Then let's give it attention. Treat it like a naughty child that has tantrums. I didn't want to dabble in Ouija boards or hold a séance but let's just talk to it. I know, I know, it sounds nuts but what else were we to do?

Sarah: In work that day I cried so much, my manager took me to one side and said and she thought that someone had died or that John and I'd had a row or we'd split up. I said I was just stressed and things were tough on us. We finished work and walking home, as we were near the house, it's already dark; it gets dark around five that time of year and it was about five thirty; John said to me, simply smile and be brave. I have to say I was beyond the ability to smile and be positive but now telling you, in hindsight, it was a good thing for John to say. He suffered so much with anxiety and depression, yet he was determined we could get over this during the time it took for us to get out. We got through the front door and into the living room; I was always frightened that there would a figure stood there, imagine the feeling of dread you would have if every time you opened your front door you expected something terrible to be waiting for you. It would make you a wreck so John flicks on the light and in a big cheery voice said *"Hello, we're home"*

John: I just started talking to it, talking out loud asking if it had had a nice day, how excited we were to be home and how great it was that we were sharing this amazing house together. I bet people are laughing at that, but what are you going to do? Get Chuck Norris with a crucifix in? No.

Sarah: John was walking around the house just talking like there was someone there, the same way you would if you went over to a friend's house. I was still terrified as you just didn't know what to expect and our poor cat was stuck in there 24/7. If that cat could talk I bet he could tell some stories. John lights some incense sticks, puts on all the lamps and puts the kettle on and looked over at me and said with this big dumb grin of his *"green tea?"* I just started laughing and crying and gave him a big hug.

John: You have no idea how anxious we were before bed but we both made a point of saying things like *"goodnight"*, *"see you in the morning"* and I said *"Try and keep it down if you can."*

Sarah: And that night not a peep.

John: Nothing at all happened that night, even the bathroom seemed warmer and less threatening. Either the entity had exhausted itself with its antics the night before or by just acknowledging it had miraculously worked.

Sarah: We both went to work, a bit more refreshed and brighter the next day and it stopped for quite a bit.

John: It got to the stage that I was happy to be nice to it; I'd do daft things like ask if it wanted a tea, say things like *"right I'm off to the loo, you stay out here."* Just silly stuff but it was working and the house seemed really nice in that it was how a house should be. I was anxious as Sarah had a few weekends away before Christmas for parties and girls nights out but I felt a bit more relaxed about the house.

Sarah: We had friends coming over one weekend and then I was away for a few weekends. I felt guilty for leaving John behind but he seemed more in control. He was less depressed and was not drinking as much and the house was behaving. I thought it would be ok, he reassured me that he and Lucky would be fine and to enjoy myself.

John: One day I was out and about in the garden and under the shed I noticed all these little bones. I thought it was a rat's nest and I hate rats, I'm terrified of them.

When I was little about six or seven my aunty and her friend took me daffodil picking at this old ruined cottage down the lane near her house, thrilling I know. While they were picking, I went into the old cottage and the floor looked like it was moving. It was full of rats, I fell down the steps and fell face first amongst them. They all scurried around me and over me as they tried to escape. It scared me. I can't abide them even though they did nothing wrong or bit me or anything. If I was a billionaire now I would probably be a super hero called RATMAN. Anyway, I tell Sarah and she says she will call pest control or the council or whoever it was to sort them out.

Sarah: We were leaving the house one Saturday morning to go shopping and we bump into the lady who lives next door. We never saw her or her husband as they both work nights and occasionally we see them leaving or arriving from work. We start chatting and she welcomes us and says if we need anything to just pop in but they mainly sleep all day and work nights, she was nice and polite and friendly. She starts talking to us about how lovely the house is and how deceptively large the garden is.

John: We are talking about the house and garden, I say it's lovely but we have found some little friends and the council are coming to sort them out and I was referring to the rats.

Sarah: John was talking about the rats in the shed and the woman obviously had misunderstood and she frowned and *asked "What, the council are taking care of it?"* and John said that they were, that they were coming on Monday. The woman looked dumfounded and John said *"Rats, we got rats."* And she went *"Oh! I thought you meant the ghosts."*

John: I said *"What do you mean?"* I was shaking; it was like I had been punched in the stomach. The woman said that at one time our houses had been one house and that our side was haunted by a woman and possibly a child but on their side, in their home, they had a very, very powerful haunting. It was a man who was angry all the time, she believed that all the spirits did cross over into both houses. I couldn't believe it. Part of me was relieved as we were not alone and we were not mad, but knowing that it was real made it more frightening if that makes sense?

Sarah: She told us that when they first moved in, there was this weird blurry object moving around downstairs that you could not look at it directly. The object was about six and a half maybe even seven feet tall. I was stunned and I told her we had the same but it was small, maybe two or three feet tall, she said that we were lucky and that was probably just the child.

John: Being told a child is haunting your home is one of the most miserable and dismal things I have ever been told plus their shadow, blur thing was seven feet tall! I don't know what was worse! I felt so sorry for our neighbours.

Sarah: At one stage I started giggling when we were comparing the antics, the cold spots, check. Footsteps, yep, ours does that. That there is a menacing feeling that something is watching you when on the loo or having a shower, check. Thinking you have been burgled in the night, tick that one off. It was almost a relief to be discussing it with someone who understood, who could relate to what we were experiencing.

John: Then she told us that one night her husband had been sat there on his own and he saw what seemed to be the outline of a very tall man, very slowly come down the stairs, almost one step at a time, very deliberately. It then entered their living room area, stood there for a few seconds like it was surveying the room and it just moved and sat in the arm chair opposite him, like it was just staring at him. This thing had no discernible features, just a shadowy outline and this was with the light on! The poor guy freaked and ran out of the house and called his bother and would not go in at all! It was bad enough with everything that had happened that I could not handle that. I asked her how they coped, how she was so calm about it and her advice was get a night job or don't be in the house at night. She said on days off they would go and stay with friends and that they were currently looking to rent out the place. It got so bad that her and husband nearly spilt up as the pressure was so intense. They called it the angry man as it would go mad in the night slamming doors, and cupboards. If they have ironed some clothes and hung them up then literally a few minutes later they would all be in a pile on the floor. It smashed a picture of her husband's parents which really upset them. They claimed it had smashed plates and cups in the night. We were fortunate as that hadn't happened to us. I made a joke that perhaps the ghost was Greek and no one laughed.

Sarah: I told her that John has started talking to it, treating it like it was part of the family and that we're house mates in a way. The woman smiled and said if it worked then great but normally it would go quiet for a while as it was re-charging getting ready to do its next thing. She had read books and been online and looked into ghosts and spirits, she said that the night we thought someone had broken in took a lot of energy for the spirit to do and it would need more energy to manifest.

John: I was cross, I believed that we were treating it with respect and that's all it needed. Deep down I hoped all these ghosts would just piss off into hers if she was working nights and party it up, but that was a wrong thing to wish. This poor woman and her husband had been traumatised just like we were and they thought that we were the lucky ones! They had to work their entire lives around it just to stay together. Those poor, poor people, I feel sorry for them.

Sarah: A problem shared is a problem halved, I guess. We chatted for about an hour and we all had to go and John and I walked into town and I knew he was furious. He needed to believe what we were doing was working and that we had everything under control. We went shopping as our friends were coming over in the evening to stay and John hit the wine aisle. I thought, no, please don't lose it, not now, not when we felt like we were winning. As soon as we got home he started on the wine and he looked sullen. He looked just like the woman who used to own this house, the woman in August with the child, he looked like he had surrendered.

Rob and Emma are the friends in question that stayed that evening with John and Sarah. I was fortunate and grateful that they both gave the time to participate in the investigative interviews. Both currently reside in England and that night is still clear in their minds even after a decade has passed since the incident. Here is their account of what they believed happened that night

Emma: I've been friends with Sarah for years, since primary school, and when I went to university I met Rob and we settled down away. We were down for a few weeks in Pembrokeshire for Christmas and Sarah said to stay over one weekend, see the house. She sounded really down, I thought maybe her and John were having relationship issues.

Rob: I met John and Sarah at the odd wedding and get together and I liked them both. John was easy going, one of those guys that will make you feel welcome and after a few hours you feel like you've known him for ever. That year we decided that we would be staying with Emma's family as we had stayed with mine the year before. I thought it would be nice to have a "session" with John and Sarah.

Emma: We got to this nice little terraced house, small on the outside but had an abundance of character. Sarah answered the door and she gave me the biggest hug ever, I thought she was going to break my ribs! As I said I've known her for years and she is a very confident and strong person but she seemed vulnerable that day. We walked inside this lovely hose, it was deceptively large and the outside did not do it justice. I loved the fireplace and the way the house just stretched so far back. John was there in the kitchen and I have to say he was steaming.

Rob: John was hammered! I laughed as he staggered out with a big glass of wine in one hand and half a bottle of wine in the other. Sarah just put a brave face on but you could sense she was furious with him.

Emma: I thought, Christ John, its 4pm and you're a mess.

Rob: He was still chatty though, his words slurred but he asked us how we were and if we wanted a drink. I thought when in Rome and John and I headed into the kitchen and he just handed me a bottle of wine and said to crack on with that.

Emma: Sarah said she would show me around the house, it was really nice and we went up to the bedroom and she closed the door and started crying. She was sat on the bed and I just hugged her and she shook and sobbed and I said what's wrong? She said she couldn't live in the house anymore. My first reaction was that she and John had not been getting along; maybe they'd had a big bust up that day hence John hitting the wine so early. This was not my friend that I had seen grow up to be so strong, this was not the friend who called me a few months previously, so excited and proud, to say John and her were buying a house. She looked thin and pale, a shell of the vibrant person I knew.

Rob: John was fine downstairs; he asked me about work and how Em's and I were getting on. He told some jokes and he just kept drinking.

Emma: Sarah told me that it wasn't John so much but the house, the house was ruining them. Again I thought, Bills, the pressure of living together, you know all of the issues you get when you settle down? But Sarah said that there was something wrong with the house and she didn't know what to do and John had given up and no one would believe her and we were scared. I tried to reassure her but we were at crossed purposes and then she angrily shouted; *"It's Haunted Em, it's fucking haunted"* and cried hysterically.

Rob: Emma was up stairs chatting with Sarah and I said could I use the toilet and John pointed at it and slurred *"In there, but it's haunted"* then he laughed his head off. I just thought it was John being John and he meant that it was haunted as he had been in there earlier and had made a bad smell or something.

Emma: She told me everything that had happened and I will tell you know that was something I didn't believe in. I told her that everything has a rational explanation but she said *"Not this time."* I did not feel anxious or frightened and I told her that if the house was haunted that Rob and I were here now and if anything happened in the night that we would find an explanation for it and if by some weird chance it was haunted then we would look for a solution. Colour returned to her face and she thanked me over and over. Sarah composed herself and we went back downstairs.

Rob: We had a good night, Sarah cooked us a wonderful meal, such an amazing cook and John kept the wine flowing and it was fun. We played board games and had some music on and had a laugh. How John can drink so much is an incredible feat. He was steaming when we got there and by eleven or twelve that night he had polished off another two bottles, maybe three, but he was still chatty and having a laugh. I think I would have been sick.

Emma: It was a good night. Sarah was more relaxed and she and John seemed happy together. Rob at this time had no idea what had been happening in the house so he thought it was just a usual night. John drank a very serious amount, I was worried, but it's his life. Around midnight or one, it was late, we called it a day and all of us were the worse for wear. Sarah shows us the den where we were to be sleeping on the bed sofa. I knew what happened to her nephew in there and I was not scared at all. In fact I liked the idea that I would be an investigator and I might find an explanation and Sarah would be happy. I didn't tell Rob at all as it was between Sarah and I.

Rob: I had no idea what had been happening at the house. We went to bed and I could hear Sarah saying to John that he'd had enough to drink and it was time for bed. John was saying one more and then he would be up and Sarah was telling him off saying that he was going to spend all night drinking and then be hung over and grumpy the next day. I heard someone storm up the stairs and I presumed that was Sarah.

Emma: I heard the main bedroom door close and downstairs I could hear the cupboard or a fridge open and a glass clink. I thought *"Ah John is on an all-nighter then?"* and I felt sorry for Sarah. Anyway I must have dropped off as I woke to hear John talking quite loudly downstairs and I thought Sarah had got up to try and get him to bed. I sat up and Rob was already wake and he whispered *"He has been talking to someone for ten minutes."* I quietly asked was it Sarah and he said he didn't think so and I then asked was John on the phone.

Rob: I knew nothing about the house at this time but I could hear John saying things like *"We live here now."* And *"We have to try and live together, we're really scared by you."* And I thought he was on the phone. I looked at my watch and it was around 3am.

Emma: I thought he must have been on the phone as I could only hear him talking, he was pleading at one stage, saying that Sarah was his world and he was losing her and that they had nowhere else to go.

Rob: John said something like *"Please, just leave us"* and this voice like an old angry woman shouted *"YOU LEAVE!"* I heard John start to cry and Emma told me to get up and see if he was OK I didn't fancy it to be honest, it was none of my business.

Emma: As John was talking this woman's voice, raspy and old, very welsh started to shout over him and you could hear John crying. I told Rob to get up and find out what was going on. Who the hell was in the house at 3am? Was it a neighbour or a family member? I clearly heard an old lady shouting at John.

Rob: I banged my head standing up in the spare room but made my way to the door and onto the landing, from there you could hear John crying and talking more clearly. He was saying things between sobs like *"You evil old Bitch"* and *"You selfish fuck."* And I heard the voice again interrupt him and say *"GET OUT!"* I cleared the stairs in next to no time and John was passed out, asleep on the settee down there. There was no one else down there at all apart from John. I even checked the front door and the back door.

Emma: Where Rob made his way down you could hear John shouting at this woman and the woman telling him to get out but Rob said that John was passed out on the Settee. I got up and John was passed out, snoring heavily. It took Rob ages to wake him up and he looked all bleary eyed and drunk and said *"what time is it?"*

Rob: I don't know if it was a prank by John, but the old woman sounded like she was a few feet from the bottom of the stairs and John was over by the storage unit. I was shocked to see him passed out, we went back to bed and left him there.

Emma: In the morning I told Sarah who hadn't heard a thing and I asked her straight was all this ghost shit a prank and if it was that I didn't find it funny especially at three in the morning. She in all fairness looked genuinely confused and she started crying saying that didn't know what had happened and had no idea what John had been up too. I don't know if there was someone in there with John, or if it had been a recording but it was a strange night. John and Sarah swore it was nothing to do with them and at breakfast we were all quiet. I told Sarah that we would stay at my mums that night instead of going out for dinner and staying again, Sarah was aghast and pleaded that we stay. John said he had no idea what had happened and whatever it was that he was sorry and that he would keep sober that night. We left and it was until about a year later that Sarah and I started talking properly again. She is convinced that something happened in that house but it's not for me to say what is haunted or not haunted. I've had no experiences or seen anything that would make me believe any differently. Psychological issues, tiredness, booze, smoking pot, all these things can make people believe in things that aren't there. I never went back to the house when Sarah lived there but I would walk back in there tomorrow and not bat an eye lid.

Rob: It was only afterwards that Emma told me about what had been happening there. She wouldn't have any of it, but I heard two distinct people downstairs and John's voice was anguished and the way the old woman shouted at him does chill me. I liked John and I miss him but hey that's life.

John: I have no idea what happened that night. Last thing I remember was getting another bottle from the Kitchen after everyone had gone to bed, I drank that and passed out. I don't remember having a conversation or row with an old woman and if that is what Rob and Em's heard then that's what they heard but I swear to you now and to anyone out there that I hope reads this and makes sense of it all, that I did not hoax it or have a recording or get someone to come into our house at 3am to piss about. We had enough on our plate without all that added to it, I got drunk and I passed out and then everyone shouted at me and blamed me.

Sarah: I didn't hear anything, when Em's and Rob left I knew I'd had enough, enough of the house, of working to keep it all together and most of all I had enough of John. I hated him, I hated him so much. If he hadn't got drunk that day and just come to bed then maybe all that wouldn't have happened. Maybe, if he hadn't been so weak and selfish and crawled into his bottle like a coward because our neighbour told him something that he didn't like or agree with, then that night would not have happened. Emma and I would not have fallen out for a year and maybe things could have got better. I made a conscious effort that day to change my life.

John: Sarah was mad about that day and the drinking, not just that night but in general. I saw coldness in her eyes, she had cut me loose. I was just some pathetic drunk, not man enough to support her and help her deal with this. I'm not looking for the sympathetic vote but anyone out there that has become dependent on alcohol when they are stressed or anxious, will understand how I felt. I felt so helpless, it was not as if I could just click my fingers and go back in time. If I could do things differently then, yes, I would but at the time the wine and the drink was my coping mechanism. I don't drink at all now, too little too late I guess. Until you have lived in that situation with everything as berserk as it was then no one can tell me how to cope or how to behave. I honestly hope that if someone out there reads this and is experiencing the same as we did then at least use this as a cautionary tale. Just get out, just leave. Stay with friends, family or even sleep in a car but don't stay and be a victim. You can't beat it, you cannot win. It chooses when it's done and we can't understand its agenda or its end game. The sad thing was is that wasn't the end, there was more in store for us.

Sarah: I didn't speak to him much at all that week. It was awful, I saw him in work and I saw him at home. He tried to talk to me on the Sunday and Monday and I just blanked him. He slept in the den with the light on. I was furious with him and I was out that weekend with friends and I wouldn't be back until Sunday night and I didn't care what happened to him and the house.

John: She really turned the screw on me and I tried to talk things through, she was having none of it. You know what? Nothing happened in the house that week, nothing at all. It was like it was enjoying the tension between us, it was happy to see us fall apart.

Sarah: On the Friday, I left straight from work with my friend. I didn't text John or even call him that weekend.

John: When she went off that Friday, my first plan was to get hammered. Hit the Wine aisle...fuck it! What's the point? But I thought no, I would sober up and when Sarah came back Sunday night the house would be clean and tidy and I would be sober and in control. The house would be the way it was when I was acknowledging the spirit, entity whatever it was. I was scared of being on my own, especially after our friends had been telling us I had been arguing with some old woman in the middle of the night. Plus, it hadn't been that long that we thought we had been burgled. My plan was just to keep it together till Sarah came home plus I had Lucky the cat to keep me company too. She needed a break and I hoped she would come home, regretful and sorry that we had fallen apart and we'd try even harder this time. This time, I would sober up. Friday night nothing happened apart from the feeling in the bathroom again and I just said *"Night night now, sleep well"* and I went to bed and kept the light and Radio 4 on. I Woke up and dawn was breaking and I was happy. I had survived the night. I had breakfast and nipped into Haverfordwest, got a few bits and bobs and thought I would cook a dinner for Sarah and me for Sunday night. I text her but had no reply. I felt so sad inside but I just hoped she was OK and we'd talk about it when she came home. That night I watched some T.V and then I was sat at the dining table reading a book and drinking green tea. Yeah, look at me all civilised and sober! I'm reading with some music quietly in the background, it was *Melody A.M* by *Royksopp,* a nice chilled album. I had text Sarah again but nothing. It's about 10pm and I hear footsteps in the den and I was thinking *"No, no, not now"* and it was the same as before, like ladies heels. It started at the end where the boiler door was and made its way to the other side. Then back and slowly and clearly it slammed what could only be the boiler door three times, Bam...Bam...Bam. I sat there staring at the ceiling with my hairs on end. Nothing happened for ages. Then slowly the footsteps started back across the den, very, very slowly. They got to where the den door was and I heard the latch go and the door swing open. For whatever reason, rather than run into the street or something I rushed to the bottom of the stairs and at the top of the landing was Lucky, he had made himself all big, hair standing up, hissing at something. I managed to call *"Lucky"*, he bolted down the stairs and hid behind the settee. I ran too and stood by the living room door that led to the hall, front door and the safety of the street. My heart was pounding in my head. I went outside on the street for a bit and paced about. A few people walked passed on the way into or out of town. I got myself together, went back in and turned the TV on. It was as loud as I could get it, made sure all the downstairs lights were on and sat bolt upright on the settee. Over the din of the TV I could hear what sounded like the upstairs being turned upside down. I heard multiple footsteps running around in the den, the latch and the doors opening and closing. I don't think I have ever felt so alone and miserable in my life. It only lasted maybe thirty seconds, maybe a bit more. I cried so much that night. I wanted Sarah home.

Sarah: I don't know exactly what happened to John that night, but when I came home Sunday he tried to act casual. He tried to hug me and be nice, but I'd had a great weekend. I felt free and fresh and young and excited again. I came back to the "ball and chain" that was John and the house. He made me feel sick. I know he tried and he'd made dinner and claimed not to have drunk all weekend but my eyes had been opened. New things were starting to come into my life and it was too late for John and me. He briefly spoke about that night, much later on and it sounded awful but part of me still blames him anyway.

John: I know Sarah blames me for so much, but I don't know how I got ghosts into the house or how drinking wine conjures up poltergeist activity? If I could do that then I would be a millionaire or working for the CIA It was already there and she wanted the house so badly. Her friend should have bloody well told her it was haunted. Ask yourself would you not buy a house because someone said it's haunted? Of course not, it's ludicrous and I'm sad that it all went wrong for us but I do blame the house. People can say *"Yeah, but you were pissed all the time"*. I....we, were happy before in the flat, I'm sure we were.

You can't unravel what's already been done but we were happy back then before that awful, miserable house.

Sarah: It was probably the worst Christmas you could imagine. We put no decorations up and John was pardon the pun, like a ghost. I guess he tried to put a brave face on it, but we were essentially over. Every opportunity I could, I spent away. Was I Selfish? Perhaps, but John had just as much chance to stay away. One night, I was in bed and he was lying on the sofa in a sleeping bag, sobbing, and I thought *"Just grow up, stop being such a child."*

John: I have wonderful and remarkable friends, but back then they had young families. They were always kind and offering to let me stay over, but it's their time. They don't need some sad, lonely man ruining their Christmas and I don't have much of a family. I just hoped Sarah and I could work it through. I wasn't stupid; I knew she was staying with other men. I just hoped I would wake up and it had all been a nightmare and we would be back in the flat, it would be summer again and we would never, ever leave.

Sarah: John was acting strange. I was going to stay with my parents for Christmas Day and on Christmas Eve; John gives me a load of presents like everything was ok. Then out of the blue, he put out a mince pie and a glass of sherry. Not for Father Christmas, no, that would have been perfectly acceptable. No, he put it out for the ghost. He even wrote it a card.

John: I just thought maybe the house would have appreciated it. People are probably laughing; it's actually one of the few things from that time that I laugh about to this day. I was hoping to find some ectoplasm in my stocking. I didn't see much of Sarah over Christmas and I just spent it on my own. I didn't drink; I swear, I just text her each day and hoped she would let me back in, back into her thoughts. I just hoped she would let me back into her heart. I was empty and heart broken, that hollow hurt in your stomach just below your chest. It's so sad. It was the first time I had been hurt by someone, it was terrible. You think, you wish you could go to sleep and wake up and be someone else, someone better or at least not wake up at all. Sadly some people out there will know how that feels. There was not a peep from the house, nothing, it was like it was just watching, and observing me as I became more and more entrenched in my depression.

Sarah: I came back the day after New Year's Eve. I decided John had to leave and I would keep the house on till we could rent it out. I came back early and John was not in the house, he'd left a note saying he was going to spend a night with his friends in Neyland. I was happy with that, they were good to him. It gave me more time working out how I was going to talk to him about everything. I was planning to effectively throw him out of his own home. A friend of mine had explained to me my entitlement and basically, John didn't really have a leg to stand on, he was broke so there was no way he could fight me legally. I must sound like a right cow, but people have no idea how tough it was on me back then. I'd fed the cat and was on the mobile chatting to this guy I had met over Christmas and I lit a candle on the mantelpiece. The mantelpiece was massive and an old fashioned brick style; it had probably been there from when the house was built. In the centre was this antique candlestick John had got from this old place on the High Street. I went into the Kitchen and poured myself a glass of wine, I was surprised that John had left any. I turned back and the living room was full of smoke, I dashed in and a waste paper basket we used to keep incense sticks in was on fire and right in the middle was the candle. I ran into the kitchen and soaked a dish cloth and put the fire out. I opened the windows and then the smoke alarm went off. I was shaking, somehow the candle had fallen out of the candle stick, rolled three maybe four feet along the top of the mantelpiece and leaping a foot or two and landing in the waste paper basket. I knew deep down what it was. What if I had gone upstairs or to the bathroom? I could have been killed.

John: I didn't know at the time what had happened until a day later. It terrifies me now. Bangs, footsteps and cold spots and the like are one thing. This sounded too strange to just be an accident. Maybe it was pissed off with Sarah or maybe it was mad that I didn't spend the night there. The day after my friends dropped me off in Haverfordwest, I walked past this shop where I bought incense sticks and popped in. They were doing fortunes or Tarot that day, I'm having a browse and this woman says *"You have a very dark shadow following you."* I thought, how charming. I asked her what she meant by that? She explained to me that she was a psychic medium. Immediately I thought, not now, not interested, not after what had happened with the blessing and what a spectacular disaster that had been. I gave the woman the time of day though, just because I needed all the help I could get back then. Suddenly, she went all gypsy fortune teller on me and said that I had spoken to the woman whose spirit resided in the house, that it was not her but one of the child spirits that had set fire to the house but it had been an accident. I thought what was she was on about? There had been no fire. It's obvious now but I hadn't been home yet and I hadn't spoken to Sarah. I told her about the night when my friends had heard me have a conversation with what sounded like an old lady. The woman didn't seem to be surprised; she didn't look at me like I had two heads. She then said it was a woman and two children and that a very hateful man would sometimes enter the house. He was the scary one, the one who made all the noise. She had me engrossed and I bought into what she was saying. I asked her what could I do and she said to buy this crystal, glass, thing and she said to wash it and place it on the mantelpiece. I didn't tell her we already had one, but being psychic she no doubt knew anyway and that the spirits would use it to muster enough energy to leave. What did I have to lose? Well, forty quid but it had to be worth it. If it got rid of the spirits or should I say help the spirits leave for a higher spiritual plain then maybe I could get Sarah back. I ran home that day, hopeful.

Sarah: I decided not to stay that night after the candle, fed the animals and stayed at a friend's. He picked me up and as he drove off he said that he thought he saw a little girl wave from the window. I told him he must have been imagining things. The next day I get home and a few minutes after I get in, John barges in all excited, babbling that everything was going to be OK. He tried to hug me but I told him to back off, he told me about this woman and what she'd said and he showed me this big green crystal.

John: I ran into the kitchen and washed it as the woman had told me to do and placed it on the mantelpiece. I knew, I just knew that this would work, I just needed Sarah to give me some time. I thought it had to be worth something to her. I needed her to have some fight, just a little, enough to give this and us, a chance. If not then let's call it a day, but in life you got to fight for what's worth living for, for what makes you happy, the things that makes you glad to be alive.

Sarah: John practically got on his hands and knees and begged me to just give him a week, to give us a week and he swore that everything that was happening in the house would stop. I told him he had a week to find somewhere else to live as we were finished and I'd met someone else.

John: I remember her telling me. You have this feeling, all the way from the base of your spine, all the way to the pit of your stomach. It felt like I had been gutted, probably where the expression comes from. It's crippling, it's everything in one big glorious ball of shit. It was anger, denial, jealousy, bitterness and a childlike feeling of just wanting to hide and cry. It had taken just three months in the house for it to end. I was furious, I demanded to know who it was, promised I would ruin whoever it was. It was Just words as it was too late. It was over.

Sarah: I explained to John what would be happening, that he would leave and I would stay a short time, told him what he had to do and he put up no fight. A week later he was back at his Dad's and then he signed the house over to me and gave me his key. He took his things; he didn't have much to be honest.

John: That last week was heart-breaking but I was right, that woman in the shop was right; the house was quiet, not a cold spot, or a feeling of menace or a footstep in the night. The crystal works. I can't explain to you how, but it works. I read afterwards that you can surround or fill an object with positive energy and create a powerful talisman to protect you. You could do it with a button if you believed in it enough.

Sarah: The night John left I was sad, but it was no good to either of us to live together but the house had been peaceful that week, serene almost. I felt that we could move on with our lives that we'd both be OK and in time maybe we could be friends. Whatever John had been on about regarding the ghosts moving on was right. Then I was in store for the worst night of my life. I went to bed at around ten. The house was quiet, warm and cosy. I read for a bit, text a bit and I dropped off. I woke up and the bedroom door was wide open. I had fallen asleep with the light on and I could have sworn I'd closed the door. Then I felt the most chilling and intense coldness I ever experienced, I could see my breath in front of my face. Then I felt the duvet slowly start to slip away from me. I held it tight and pulled it up to my chin and then something grabbed my foot and pulled.....I....I screamed and screamed. I screamed for John.

John: It all started up again the night I left. It was probably because I took that crystal with me. It cost me forty quid. I'm sure her new bloke could get her a new one. He seemed to be giving her plenty of other things if you know what I mean.

Sarah: It was awful. Everything was intensified. This was no nightmare or hallucination. It grabbed me. I hardly spent a night there since. I moved out and luckily not too long afterwards I managed to rent the place out but people don't stay long. Thankfully they've been contractors from the refineries or students from the college. Now and again when someone asks to terminate their tenancy after only a few months, deep down I know why, but I never ask and I never mention it when new people come to view the property. I know how that woman must have felt when John and I came to view the property that day. She must have been so relieved to leave. There was not a chance in hell that she was going to mention it and neither am I. Some close friends have said that I am obliged, that I should tell people, but really? Would anyone out there believe it if they were told a house was so haunted that it might destroy their lives? No, you would look insane. I need the money as the mortgage won't pay itself. You asked me earlier about the people that live their now and you asked me was it my responsibility to protect them, to tell them, for all I know the house might have stopped or they might be happy there. It's not for me to say and even if they ask then I will say no that I don't know what they are on about. You can't blame me for that. I don't speak much to John, I dropped him a message when you got in touch, when I saw your letter and I have a family now and happily married. What happened before is just a small part of my life. You move on and in time you start to forget, it's only natural to move on. I can't give anyone an explanation of what was happening at that house. Some people have easy answers but they aren't there. Some will say that it's made up, made up for what? So I can look like a nutter? Made up so that I can't live in my house? It was very real to me and it totally fucked John up. All we have to do is look back and be relieved that it's over. Its done; apart from a few visits a year I have very little to do with the House.

John: Ten years is a long time. I try not to pass the house if I can help it. I know it's haunted, it is, really. OK you can say: define a haunting. You see movies now like paranormal activity, with demons, movies about aliens. But a haunting to me, is when something beyond our understanding inhabits a home, the people in it can't comprehend what is happening. There is no solution, no help, and no magic wand to make it leave. Science and religion can't make it stop; it's a powerful force that no one can persuade to leave. It holds all the cards. I can't think of a rational explanation for such an intense and traumatic experience. It was prolonged and it was at times, truly terrifying. It drove Sarah and I apart. She and I are the ghosts now. Do you know, I saw her the other day, by chance in the street and we said a quiet hello and kept walking, we are strangers. There is no bond there, no connection. It used to make me sad thinking of how happy we were and how complete my life felt, now it's nothing more than a dark memory. I don't regret losing the house, not in the slightest. I am blessed to have no ties to that place; I was just another plaything or victim to the entity, depending on how you look at it. When I left and went back to my dad's, I worried that it would follow me but I have moved plenty in the last ten years and I make sure that I always have that piece of green crystal with me. I never want that thing back in my life. I will never step foot in that house again as long as I live and I genuinely hope and pray that whoever is living there now has a much easier time than us. You've got to ask yourself all these couples having a terrible time of it, arguing all the time. Maybe, just maybe it's because of entities, spirits, whatever you want to call them. There, driving them apart for whatever reason these things do it for. We can't fathom their motives. I took hundreds of photos while I was there and nothing showed up. We had the house blessed and it made it worse. People came to our home and were badly affected. There is no safety in numbers. Science can't explain it. You're dealing with something on an entirely different level. If this is happening to you then get out, get out now. You can't fight it, you won't win and you'll end up losing everything that matters to you. If you hear our story, don't be harsh on us and call us frauds or weirdo's and if it does happen to you or it's happening then like I say, just get out, get out before it's too late and you lose everything.

***

I hope the transcripts have given you much food for thought as it has for me and apologies if the events described have insulted your beliefs, played on your mind or even chilled you. The purpose of this was for you to come to your own conclusion. Your own philosophies and beliefs will have already kicked in and some of you will have explanations of some sort while others may have experienced similar occurrences and may feel a sense of understanding, dread or sympathy for the people involved. To some of you, it is just a story.

I have spent much time pondering this case but without a solid investigation at the location it is impossible to determine an explanation. The gentleman involved did allow me to examine the photo's he took while the events unfolded and while nothing obvious was apparent they do warrant further intensive research and scrutiny to see if there is any paranormal activity recorded.

I have spoken to scores of people involved in all manner of paranormal events but John and Sarah were the ones that displayed a full spectrum of emotion and a genuine dread in the recanting of their experiences which to this investigator I believed to be genuine. It may be an elaborate hoax, and if so then it has been played masterfully and with the other witness's interviewed also acting out their part very well and with utter conviction.

I have several theories, none of which I trust you will understand, I can publish at this time as I don't have the hard facts. I do believe that John, Sarah and the others involved did experience something there, whether it was paranormal or psychologically induced by an outside factor would require a much more intensive investigation.

How many people out there, perhaps you yourself, reading this have experienced something unexplainable at home? Those noises and chills that worry you or a blurry image seen for a second in the corner of your eye. Is it explainable or is there more behind the veil of our reality? I ask both the sceptic and the believer that when you hear noises in the night, are you quick to have an explanation? What do you base your assumptions on? Will we ever have the answers? Perhaps when we finally pass on, when our life comes to an end, will there be nothing or a perhaps a whole new existence that as humans, we cannot fathom?

I hope you have enjoyed this and there is much, much more that in the future I will publish. I have had a long and varied career in paranormal research and you can contact me at: paranormalchronicles@aol.com, should you wish to offer any theories on this case or perhaps the subject in general. Perhaps you have your own experience, or perhaps have experienced or are experiencing something very similar to John and Sarah's case.

I will leave you with one final part of this tale. John in one of his attempts to prove that there was an entity haunting the house was able to record with his mobile phone a ten second audio clip. It on first listening appears to have nothing of consequence just some ordinary background noises but run through an audio filter you can just make out, very quietly, but discernible the sound of a child singing.

Thank you for reading and sleep well.

The author would like to note that the Paranormal is a very sensitive subject and has appreciated your commitment to reading this novel. If you would like to contact him regarding anything that has been written about in this novel or for general information then please do so by emailing: paranormalchronicles@aim.com and will always appreciate any feedback, views, opinions, theories, beliefs and philosophies in a respectful and understanding manner. Please take the time to review this kindle title on Amazon.

If you enjoyed this then two new paranormal chronicles are in progress and will be due out in 2014.

Please feel free to recommend to a friend that enjoys the subject of the Paranormal.

Thank you.

A most haunted house © G L Davies 2013

NOW AVAILABLE ON KINDLE

GHOST SEX: THE VIOLATION by G L Davies

Ghost sex The Violation is the terrifying and disturbing follow up to the worldwide bestselling *a most haunted house*. This true and chilling account centres on a family in Pembroke Dock, West Wales that are invaded by a brutal paranormal presence. The home is subjected to a prolonged and frightening haunting and escalates to a sickening and disturbing series of sexual violations.

Paranormal Investigator G L Davies conducts a series of interviews with three generations of family that have been deeply affected by the vile supernatural intrusion into their lives. If you think you know about paranormal encounters, if you think this is just a Welsh version of the Entity or a more sexually descriptive version of the potter's wheel scene in Ghost, then you are asked to reconsider and push away any preconceptions of what you are about to read. This novel is possibly the most chilling and debase paranormal account ever published and it is not for the faint of heart. Due caution is advised.

Download now and join the investigation today and decide for yourself on what really happened to this family... and then pray it never happens to you.

Read the #1 Bestseller today

Read now on Kindle and Kindle app

Made in the USA
Middletown, DE
15 December 2016